I took my life for granted
until you came along.
I didn't value it at all
until that morning
I held you in my arms.

How ironic,
that through your death
I would learn how to live.

How ironic,
that in the relinquishing
of your body, you would
teach me how to love my own.

How ironic,
that there would be a gift
hidden in the devastation.

She Was Born

Words on Loss and Liberation

Libby June Weintraub

Cover & Book Design © Benard Creative www.benardcreative.com

Cover Image © Dylan Griffin www.dylangriffin.com

Magnolia Illustration © Joanna Szmerdt Art @elfencode

Author photo © Alice Smith @alicesmithmusic

First Edition Printed and Published by Prodon Enterprise, 2023.

Second Edition Printed and Published by BookBaby, 2023. www.bookbaby.com

Second Edition Design Update prepared by Ever Pallas www.everpallas.com

We are donating 100% of the proceeds of this book to Every Mother Counts, an organization that collaborates with critical decision-makers, thought and practice leaders, and community members worldwide to advance improvements in maternal health. They partner with local organizations that serve historically marginalized communities. Their mission is to make pregnancy and childbirth safe, equitable, and respectful for every mother everywhere. www.everymothercounts.org

Laid out in Primo Serif, a typeface designed by Danish type foundry Playtime

979-8-9851970-0-6 First Edition Paperback

979-8-9851970-1-3 Second Edition Paperback

979-8-9851970-2-0 Ebook

For Magnolia Grace and Steve

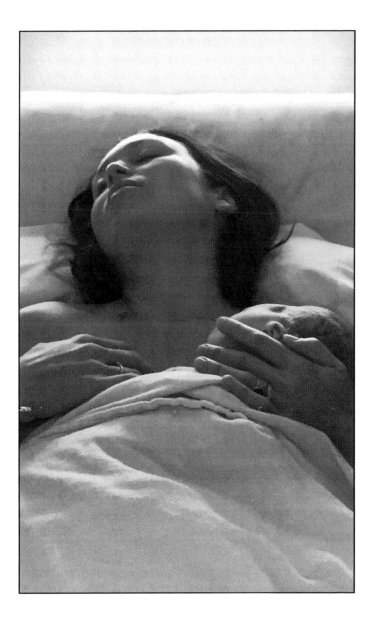

I want to talk about what happened.

Foreword

From the powerful impetus of reading my wife's collection of poems, I take pen into hand with nervous trepidation for what I am about to revisit. Here before me lies undoubtedly the most ominous, unresolved and painful mystery of my life. The still-born death of my first-born child Magnolia Grace.

I write this for myself as I continue to search and scratch for a teaching, a resolution, or even a word that offers some sense of understanding and healing in the dark realms of my mind, amidst the innumerable questions that have clouded and inhabited it since we lost her, so suddenly, just days before her due date.

I write this for parents who have experienced a similar loss and just don't know what to do with it – while they hold space for their grieving partners, and traverse the deepest pains and vacancies of their own trauma.

I write this foremost for my courageous wife Libby June, who has endured inconceivable heartbreak and healing and a life's journey of understanding which comes through in these pages. Her expression in this body of work reaches beyond the intellectual realm of straight prose, and comes through with raw honesty and profound beauty.

It dawned on me some time ago that poetry (something I could never get comfortable with writing myself) is an author's way of expressing the intangible, be it the hidden recesses of the subconscious or the mysterious expanse of Source-God itself, in such a way that human language is ill-equipped to express through the linear avenues of the mind. Such is the case when it comes to words that pertain to the loss of a child. Quite simply, for me, and others I've met, there are no words that can accurately describe or accommodate this space of devastation and longing.

In the depths of despair and all along her journey of discovery and healing, which continues to this day, my wife Libby has given voice to her experience and in the process has created a staggering collection of poems written with deep vulnerability, bravery, and beauty. Words that take the shroud away and reveal what it is like to come to terms with the death of a baby rather than move forward with a 'stiff upper lip' as many generations of parents who've suffered such loss have been urged to do. In a time where women are still encouraged to make believe it didn't happen, to just keep moving forward, encouraged to 'have another one' these words couldn't be more valuable. They give voice to an aspect of the healing process that is essential, the expression of our grief, and our journey through it.

We live in a society that encourages us to 'tough it out' to 'be strong' and 'keep it together.' This mindset is not only irrational, it is an ineffective way to deal with our grief. On the contrary what is needed is the encouragement to go deep into the darkened corners of this experience and with assistance, find healing in what lies there.

As a couple we chose to walk into the darkness together. It was frightening and messy and yet it miraculously has deepened our love and intimacy. It has framed the wonder that is life and our commitment to living it fully. It has allowed me to find (albeit bittersweet and painful at times) a profound union with Magnolia in a spiritual and intangible way. At times I miss her terribly and at other times I watch her grow up in my imagination. Through these poems I have learned that there is no shame in sharing my feelings. The teachings and essence of Magnolia's brief time, imparted within these pages, are always next to me, even though her body isn't.

I urge the reader, whatever extraordinary hardship or pain might befall you – be fearless and walk into it, in hopes of healing, and perhaps uncovering the deepest meaning of what it means to live.

Stephen (Scooter) Weintraub

Introduction

I will never forget the endless moments of connection with Magnolia, hands on my belly. The countless hours of meditation, the chanting and prayers for her healthy life. I carried her to full term. She died in my womb unexpectedly at 39- weeks from a rare condition known as a velamentous cord insertion. No one had any idea of the complication until she was stillborn.

Although our doctor detected an abnormality with her cord at our 21-week scan, in our follow up ultrasounds nothing indicated a velamentous insertion. She was strong, robust and healthy. Had we known about the complexity ahead of time, I never would have opted to turn her from her breech position at 36-weeks in order to deliver her vaginally.

I have no idea if she would be alive today had we detected the velamentous cord insertion. I have no idea if turning her with the velamentous insertion complicated things, although my sense is that it did. What I do know is that there is nothing that can be done now. All we can do is keep on moving forward knowing that we did the best we could with the information and support that we had at the time.

Depending on how I look at the past eight years of my life, I see a journey of immense tragedy and loss, or I know it to be one of deep initiation and profound healing. Some days it feels like both. Some days I am amazed that I could feel this degree of loss and still be standing. Some days I am humbled by the chaos and heartbreak that has given birth to these words. But most days I am thankful for how much I have been changed by all that has happened.

My first pregnancy ended in miscarriage at six weeks. Magnolia was stillborn a year later. Twelve months into my grieving process, my mother was diagnosed with stage four glioblastoma multiform, the most aggressive form of brain cancer. I miscarried our third pregnancy and our fourth. My mum died eighteen months later.

The book you hold in your hands is here to help evolve the culture of grief. In these pages, you'll bear witness to the beauty, the devastation and the fullness of grief, which is really just the fullness of love. After those many awkward moments, not knowing how to act, nor what to say, nor how to feel my healing has begun.

I am convinced that even though this loss has dismantled me piece by piece, the healing that was born of her death; the deepening of love and intimacy within myself and my marriage, along with these words – was the very gift she came to give.

I'm no longer willing to hide from what happened. I'm no longer willing to hide how it feels to give birth to death. My healing has begun. I am listening. I am granting grief a voice – because I am not the same person I was before her.

I remember how quiet it was in that room with my mother, as we waited, staring into that screen, waiting to hear her heart beating. The boundless possibilities of Magnolia's life dissolved into a dark, empty nothing. She was dead. Everything stopped. Everything fell away, the constant churning in my mind, the fears and concerns for her birth. In that small room the doctors words trailed off into the background. I felt a presence in that room and in my body, a still, quiet, presence I had searched my whole life for. I picked up my phone. I called Steve. I broke the news.

So many details about that day escape me, but there are moments tattooed into the fabric of this body forever. Like the moment they placed her in my arms. I remember the smell of her, like sweet grass, earth and blood. I remember the color of her skin. I remember the whisper of brown hair that covered her head. Her long eyelashes how they curled up at the end, just like her father's. Her little fingers, her oval-shaped fingernails. Her long legs and delicate feet.

Holding her in my arms softened me; it broke me open. I had never loved myself as much as I did the day she was born. I had never cared for myself like I did in the days, weeks and months that followed her death. I had never held something so precious in all my life. Stripped raw, I finally surrendered. I asked for help and I let myself receive it.

The poetry found within these pages came pouring out of me in the months that followed, arriving often in the middle of the night and refusing to leave until I scrawled them down on my lined yellow note pad. Sometimes it was her voice whispering to me from beyond the veil, encouraging me to slow down, to rest. Sometimes it was an insight from my heart. Sometimes a pining, a pleading. Writing the words down and sharing them was foundational to my healing. They were a way to feel connected to her and an attempt to share the unraveling, to make sense of the isolated island of child loss Steve and I now inhabited, and the shipwrecked debris called our life that floated aimlessly and endlessly around it.

When I emptied the words onto the page, the feelings, the energy would move – I'd hear things and understand things I didn't before. I kept a journal to Magnolia throughout my pregnancy. I wrote to her daily, mostly at night or early in the morning and I would tell her how much I loved her. Some days, I would ask her how she was feeling, what she needed from me. Then I would wait in the silence, pen in hand, hoping to hear a response. A lot of the time what I heard was a quiet voice inside. *I need you to slow down*, it would say. *I need you to rest, to take time to be with me.*

I remember laying on the couch under a warm blanket the morning we returned from the hospital. Mum was running her fingers through my hair, brushing my forehead, smoothing out my frown as she'd done hundreds, thousands of times before. And as her fingers thread through my hair, Magnolia spoke to me in the burdened space of my heart.

Let her touch you. this is how I will touch you now, through her hands. let her love you. it will be me touching you, it will be me loving you; this is how I can be with you now.

We think death is wrong. We're taught to look away. We burn or bury the body. We give ourselves days or weeks to grieve. We live in a world that rushes through things, so when death finds us, we rush through that too. Healing in a culture that worships perfection is never an easy process because healing is a messy and imperfect process.

We think we are burdened by our grief but we are burdened by our unwillingness to feel it. There were days I went from my bed, to the shower, to the back patio for a tea. There were days I would stare up at the sky, and then go back to bed. There were nights I would howl and scream, and then collapse into a deep sleep. Steve would hold me while I wailed and shook.

I remember looking in the mirror after one of my long hot showers in those timeless weeks after her death. I didn't even recognize myself. Standing naked before the mirror I felt so much compassion. I fell in love with the bloated and bleeding woman staring back at me. After all of the years spent judging and shaming myself for not being perfect and for all that had fallen apart in my life, I finally saw the women underneath, the one who had endured it all. The one who had always given her best. The one who had just lost her baby. I touched and rubbed every inch of my skin. I massaged the places that stretched to accommodate Magnolias growing limbs. I thanked my body over and over again for all she had done to create such a beautiful life, only to have to give it back so soon.

Even though eight years have passed, I still wake up some mornings with a heaviness in my heart. I still yearn for her body in my arms one more time. The difference now is that I don't push away the feelings. I have found a way to welcome them, to walk along-side this part of me that will never get over the experience of leaving the hospital without her.

No experience has been more earthshattering than the day I gave birth to Magnolia still and unmoving. Nothing has come close to the gut-wrenching moment I handed her to her father and kissed her goodbye. There are no words to describe the disappointment I felt standing motionless under the steaming hot shower at the hospital, waiting for them to take her away. Or the heartache I felt when I realized the hospital was not going to give us a birth certificate, because she wasn't alive when she was born. We think not talking about what happened will help us move on but if we want to heal, we must be willing to tell the truth about how we really feel.

I have spent the past few years shaping this book of poetry. I have searched through journals and piles of my poems scribbled on notepads, the fertile ground of my healing. I have spent hours corralling them into something worth sharing that could describe the healing that has happened. Something that would bring to life all I've learned, and at times it's felt impossible.

I am in awe of the explosiveness of my rage and the relief that has come from feeling it after all these years spent stuffing it inside. I am opened in the core of my being by the raw tenderness of my husband's vulnerability and the closeness that's been cultivated inside of our grief. It has been such a privilege to give birth to our baby, hold her in my arms, and know her now as this light that filters through our lives.

The hidden gift in this experience is that Magnolia's death became the portal through which I would finally feel all of the emotions I'd never allowed to the surface. Her birth was the catalyst for vital growth, love, and healing.

What if her sole reason for being with us for this short time was to share her love with us and allow us to share our love with her? It is hard to imagine that that could be enough, but what if it is? What if that's the point of our entire existence, our reason for being, to share our love with one another and know that that is enough?

Thank you for allowing us to share our daughter and our love of her with you, and for listening and holding our grief in your beautiful hands.

Libby June Weintraub

She Was Born

she was born
2:26am November 26th, 2014

she was
6 pounds 2 ounces

she was
21 inches long

she was
our first baby

she was
our second pregnancy

she was
breathtakingly beautiful

she was
dead

I Remember

I remember the sound his footsteps made
as he pushed me out of the hospital in the wheelchair

I remember climbing into the front seat of the car
and buckling my seatbelt

I remember looking back at my mother
she was exhausted, we were all exhausted

we drove away
empty handed

Some Unspeakable Dream

I want to hold you in my arms again
I want to imagine all of this

some terrible dream
some unspeakable dream
from which I can awaken

but I open these eyes
and you are nowhere to be found

Letter To God

when I walk past her room
when I hold him at night

my arms ache

they ache because
I cannot make sense
of the fucking mess

that has become our lives

No Path We Know

into the unknown we go
asking the unanswerable questions

before our eyes a foreign land
no path we know

grief washes over us
taking with it every comfort

taking with it any semblance
of who we once were

into the unknown we go
asking the unanswerable questions

waiting in the silence
wedged between two worlds

the one we have left behind
and the one where we find ourselves

I Want It To Be Over

I want it to be over
I want to feel free again

I don't want
to talk about the gift

I don't want
to talk about the details

I don't want
to talk about these feelings

I don't know what to say
I don't know how I feel

Running In Place

I am aware of this dull ache

it starts in my guts, twists around my heart
and curls inside my throat

it feels like a rope soaked in years of trying.

my heart pounds, I am afraid to pull it out
I am running. I am running in place

she was the most beautiful baby I've ever seen
I only show the photos where she is beautiful

the frightening ones
are hidden in a folder on my desk top

she is not frightening
how I feel when I look at her is

He Doesn't Look At Her Photo

he doesn't look at her photo anymore

it brings back too many memories
it brings back the horror of my 15-hour labor
it brings back the terror of seeing her lifeless body

it brings back the panic of not being able to change the situation
it brings back the paralysis of holding her
and not feeling her breathing
it brings back the grief that suffocates him
and the inconsolable anguish

the agony he felt when they came to take her away

he doesn't look at her photo anymore
so it sits on my desk, in a tiny gold frame
and it sits on my altar, next to a picture of my father

he doesn't look at her photo anymore
and yet, I was the one who left the room to shower
while he waited

I was the one who placed her in his arms
I was the one who couldn't bear to see her go
so I stayed under the hot water,
washing my heartache down the drain

I have never considered how heavy that must have been
I haven't put myself in his shoes on that day
and I am so ashamed,
ashamed to say that in my grief I haven't even considered
what that must have been like for him

sitting in that recovery room with my mother and our baby
waiting for them to take her away

he doesn't look at her photo anymore
and I don't blame him

I Want To Know

I pull out the weeds, I till the soil

I want to know if there is more to me
than this name, this form, this mess in my mind

I want to know if there is life
beyond this death

Everything

I walk into your room
I run my fingers over the striped cotton leggings
I hold the soft sweaters, your socks in my hands

I stand in the silence
I open the blue satin box from the hospital
I untie the bow and stare at your photo

I take out the hat you were wearing
I press it to my lips
I drink in the smell of you
I gaze at your one solitary foot print, black on white paper

I sit on the floor
I stare at the hungry caterpillar book, the bottles, your crib
I examine the crystal hanging in the window

there are tiny rainbow specks dancing across the walls
there is light in this room
I imagine you here

I hold onto these details
the story of your birth
the day I will never forget

I tell everyone who will listen,

how precious you were

how everything, everything, everything

reminds me of you

Will I Ever Make It

as these breasts of mine fill with milk
a milk that you will never taste

my heart also fills with sadness
a sadness you will never know

I wonder if you realize the harrowing grief
left in your wake

I wonder if you and God are drinking tea
praying for me to see the blessing in this

I wander from room to room
frantically searching for you

and I wonder, will I ever
make it back to shore

I Don't Feel It Anymore

I felt the life in me just weeks ago
I felt the energy growing
now I don't

I just feel the heaviness
I feel the weight
of what has died in me
I feel the weight
of what has died
and I wonder

how do we begin again
where does the courage come from
to open

how do we take that first step

A Place for the Suffering

I sit in this dark room, waiting
for the healing, the revelation

but I can't see an end to this

I bring pen to paper
to liberate the aching parts
a place for the suffering

you are a piece of my heart

and I will carry you with me
for the rest of my life

Don't Look For Me

don't look for me
in that room
for I am not there

don't look for me
in the drawers
amongst the clothes
nor the pages
of those fairytale books

the room you made
the soft toys, diapers,
clothing and crib

none of these things
point to the magnificence

when you stop
wondering
wandering
around the circles
you've traced
I am right here

don't look for me
in that room
for I am not there

I am
in the spaces
the faces
the feet walking

I am
in the noise
the wind
the sunlight
that burns

I am
in the grief
alive and shaking
not destroyed
but stronger

I am
in the air
in your lungs
in your heart
I am flowing
in your bloodstream
our intermingled cells

I am
in the laughter
his eyelashes
the wrinkled sheets
and folds of your
glorious body

there is nothing
nothing in this world
that you could do
to stop this

let it burn
like fire and sun
let it finish

what was begun
that early morning
when you birthed the body
that bore my name

let us remember
the preciousness
that lifted you anew
that removed what wasn't true

let go of your stories
so, you may see

there is nothing in this world
that could stop this love

Something of Extraordinary Value

it doesn't matter how long it takes
what matters is that you continue

what matters is that you listen
to that voice that is your own.

if you keep your focus on what was taken
you will never see what was given

that morning you gave birth to me
and laid to rest your endless wandering.

can you lay down the story
of having been wronged.

can you hold onto
this unadulterated love.

can you sit down and drink
from the wisdom inside

here, in the midst of this suffering
something of extraordinary value is found.

Speak About Your Experience

the water may look dirty
but it will quench the most barren desert
if you turn on the tap

Your Arms

when you put
your pain on the page
your arms are free
to carry something
far more exquisite

The Stillness

I have been running
in all directions
looking for God

I have tried to tame
that which desires
that which wants

I was running the day I fell pregnant
searching, even as my belly grew
for a way to touch
the peace
the quiet
the stillness

when she died
it was my own voice that came
to speak about the unspeakable

and when I held her body
the voice I had ignored all these years
comforted me
I knew in that moment
the God I so desired

the peace
the quiet
the stillness

lives inside of me
inside of this shaking
searching and stumbling

The Beginning

I remember the dark room
the soft bed, me silently praying to you

I remember the shower, the water on my skin
the heat caressing me

I remember the large blue ball filled with air
holding our weight as I rocked back and forth

I remember the cool linoleum floor beneath my feet
the worn-out cotton gown, draped soft around my body

I remember swaying back and forth
focusing, breathing, listening

I remember smiling at your fathers distressed face
hoping my love could melt it

I remember lifetimes of heaviness falling away
lifetimes of fear, your love tearing me open

in one single moment you took everything
shattering my perfect vision.

your father's lips pressed against mine
an ocean crashing between us

I felt his horror – everything taken.
I felt it, but I was too far gone.

Curriculum

there is nothing that can prepare you for this
no class, no teacher, no book

it is the most brutal curriculum

this is not the invitation I was waiting for
this is not the delivery I was expecting

but, I will say yes
I am here to learn

the most potent curriculum of the spirit

Her Ashes

the box was emerald green
its smooth edges, these fingers will never forget

inside, a clear plastic bag
filled with white and grey gravel

I placed the box on the ledge by the fireplace
I lit candles and surrounded it with an altar of flowers

I wanted the heavens to open up. I wanted to shout
we don't fucking deserve this

but it wasn't about deserving, and I knew it
even though I didn't fully understand,
something had happened in the hospital

something for which I haven't words
the love, the tears, the ecstasy of holding her

I wanted to open up that box
and scatter her all through the house
I wanted to tear open my skin
and show the world the inside of my aching

I wanted to slide slowly out of this skin and join her
but he kept me there – his love, his heart, his ache

it kept me there, walking the periphery
of this open wound

The Inextinguishable

you are afraid of your darkness
yet it is the most intoxicating part.

you are afraid of your anger
yet I prefer it to the politeness that covers.

you are afraid of your grief
yet it is honest and vital to the healing.

you are afraid of making mistakes
yet here is where life advances; in the messiness.

I feel you and your longing
to move out beyond that tiny room you've kept yourself in

you hold the key, you have touched it
you will teach others how to touch it too.

you will teach others that the gate way to the light
often comes through the grief

and to avoid the anger is to avoid the truth
and to avoid the pain is to avoid the teaching

to avoid the grief is to avoid the inextinguishable
that burns, that dances, that sees beyond the suffering.

The Revelation

what say you
of this grief?

holy.

what say you
of this rage?

holy.

what say you
of this death?

holy.

what say you of this disaster
this inability to stand
this devouring fire
the hopelessness
that scratches at my insides?

holy.

holy.

holy.

Do Trees Mourn

do trees mourn when they lose their leaves
that thought crossed my mind this morning

a thought planted there no doubt by my daughter

it's when my mind spins
that I hear her clearly, prompting me to listen

I hear her in my ear, calling me
like the autumn to let go of my leaves

did I lose her, or did I let her go
because at times it sure feels like I lost her

like the leaves of the tree
at some point I must let go of her
at some point I must let go of everything

I hear her voice
I didn't go anywhere

and just like those leaves that fall and fertilize the tree
she fertilizes my soul – she nourishes me

I dig into my roots, I pull on the earth
I trust that some purpose is unfolding

I stand naked, I bare my soul
readying myself

do trees mourn when they lose their leaves
or do they dance and sway in ecstasy readying themselves,
readying themselves for the season to come

that thought crossed my mind this morning

Raging Heart

you wander, wild, wasted
by what was taken

no longer willing
to cover the profanity
you used to hide

raging heart
now more alive

you scream and shake your fist
but know that something will come of this

for all of your reasons to give up
you have a hundred more to keep on going

perhaps the first step to healing
is letting this grief out into the world

tell me how much it hurts
instead of pretending

I Am The One

I am the one who carried you
39 weeks in my body
your beautiful limbs
fashioned from my life

I am the one
who sang to you

I am the one
who said yes

I am the one
who doesn't understand

I am the one
who wants to know

I am the one
who announced the news

I am the one
who made it beautiful

I am the one
who saw the light
in the room that night

I am the one who grieves

I am the one
who must find peace
in that empty room
filled with objects
you will never touch

I am the one who holds him
when his grieving shakes the house

I am the one
who listens and patiently waits

I am the one
who investigates
the inner turning
of this broken heart

the shards of glass
I walk across
to the door

I am the one
who opens it

I am the one
who walks outside
and looks up

I am the one
who is willing to begin again
after all of the pain
and all of the hurt
and all of the disappointment

I am the one
with the broken heart
and the shards of glass
in her feet

I am the one
who has removed those shards
piece by piece

I am the one
who carried you
nurtured you
birthed you
held you
loved you

he is the one
who kissed you
goodbye

The Truth of It All

when the mask drops to the ground
and smashes into a thousand messy pieces
I am left with myself
I am left with the grief
that is a constant pulse in my blood
in my breath

I am left with the memory of stillness
I am left with the image of her limp body lying on the table
as Alisha, Aleks and my mother bathe her

I am left with this immense longing that lives in my heart
that is lodged in my throat along with these words
these words that cannot seem to describe
the disappointment I felt
as he pushed me down the hallway past all the other mothers.

when the public face
that covers the truth of my grief falls away
I am left with the memory of my mother
with her bloodshot eyes off a 20-hour flight from Perth
waiting to meet her dead granddaughter

I am left with the tears I shed
when Steve finally decided to hold Magnolia
when he opened his shirt and clutched her to his chest.

when the mask drops to the ground
and smashes into a thousand messy pieces
I am left with the truth of it all

not the picture I have painted for you

Night After Night

I feel the pulse
where our skin touches
our fingers entwined

I dream of a child
bundled up between us
big eyes and soft skin

I massage his back
I smile knowing
the sleep that comes

I smile at this ritual

my love in these hands
my love that touches
every ache in him

when she died
Cassy and Danny gave us
a large rose quartz heart

I fell asleep every night
cradling it like the baby
I longed to hold

their hearts generosity
I will never forget
dinners and nights

food and flowers
laying on warm sheep skins
under the stars
soft chanting

the swirl of incense
this dark house

these bare feet
the wooden floor
I am here

I am doing dishes again
washing away olive oil and spices
from someone's empty plate

I am here
I know I'm here
washing, cleaning, breathing

he wraps his arms around me
his tears stain my shirt

I feel him
I know him
I love him

These Tears That Fall

these tears that fall
echo in the unspeakable silence
that fills this home

these empty walls
where you once slept so close to me

my heart could hear yours beating

these tears that fall
wash away this unfathomable

love and longing

In the Darkest Moments

I want you to know
that in the darkest moments

when your guts are twisted
and the tears, so heavy
marbled streaks of red,
laid bare across your face

your hair a hurricane of fury
this is when I love you the most.

in the moments
when you are no longer trying
to hold it together, here
is where I meet you, here
is where I feel you

when you are broken,
bruised and questioning
can I continue...

here, in this moment
this is when I love you most
this is when I love you the most.

This Is Not a Tragedy

all day I peer through the windows watching you
all afternoon, I am the wind by your side
these whispered words

don't try to control your tears, let them come
looking for answers only leads to more questions
let the words come

what if you can hear me. then what
don't let your mind tell you otherwise
you know what you know

this is not a tragedy

a tragedy, is letting this consume your life
a tragedy, is getting to the end never having recovered
a tragedy, are all the days lost in your searching

remember how the grief shattered you
uncovered the love you'd hidden from yourself

remember how grateful you were
you kept saying it, over and over

you felt the significance of what was happening
even though you didn't like it

you found beauty in that dark place
you found a freedom you'd never known
you found love

this is not a tragedy

Annihilation

even though I've never held a gun
I understand the weight of one

I understand the paralyzing sadness and the death
that no amount of talking can tend to

the truth is talking walks around things
the truth is words are insufficient

how do I explain the beauty and gift of her birth
to faces that search mine for tragedy

how do I explain the night that bled all pride from me
drained of all I thought was mine

I will never forget as I labored into the night
as she descended – my heart
her life, my mind

He Holds Me

he holds me as I erupt
a piercing fit of grief, of rage

these tears I shed are for her
and all the years I've pissed away
trying to become someone

her death gave me back my life
showed me where I was asleep
pointed to my busy life and the

worthlessness
hidden beneath

I've been treading water
in this ocean of grief
since I can remember

and I never imagined
in the depths of such pain
I could feel such relief

When the Storm Passes

sometimes I wrap his feet in hot towels
then massage them slowly with oils

sometimes he runs me a warm bath
I light candles and scatter salt into the water

now and then I leave a love letter, card or note
a hand-picked flower from the garden on his desk

mostly, he holds me and rubs my back patiently
tells me how great I am doing, how proud of us he is

often, we take long walks in silence holding hands
we lay on the grass in the backyard, on a pile of warm blankets

blown to pieces

What Is Left

what is left
when the grief
burns through me

emptiness
nothingness
quiet

Experiencing Her Now

what keeps me from experiencing her now
is the desire to keep remembering her

the way she was

the more I relive the past
the farther away from her I feel

In Every Way

I am closer to you now
 than I have ever been

I am in all things known
I am in all things seen

I am in everything
in every way

I am the rising moon
and the falling day

there will never be a moment
I'm not standing by your side

to comfort, to love you
to lead and to guide

Embracing

absurdity:
trying to make sense of things

sanity:
embracing what is

absurdity:
trying to make sense of things

sanity:
embracing what is

This Home

this home has become
a holy temple

every day people leave flowers
and food by the door

they do not knock
they do not preach
they do not disturb us.

our house has become a holy temple

My Love

you help me see
beyond what was taken

you help me hear
the music of our life again

and it is beautiful
and I am so grateful

because of you
I keep on walking

I Will Hold Her Again

I have no idea
where I am headed
but in the end
I will hold her again

if only in my mind
where I travel
upon clouds
where the light
of a thousand rainbows
finds me free

Motherhood

against my naked chest
I held her lifeless body
I dissolved into nothing

the light I couldn't find
in someone else's dogma
I saw in her beautiful face.

her death
is a holy tapestry
stitched into this body

I Will Never Forget

I will never forget you
not even for a second
shall my thoughts wander

from the beauty that you are
and the miracle you have opened
inside me

I will never forget you
not even for a second
my beautiful child

from the stars you came
upon a blazing star you left
to leave your trail

across this darkened sky

A Place That's Mine

no more hiding
no more censoring
no more sucking it up

I want to say what I need to say
I want to know what I need to know
I want to love what I need to love

I want a place that's mine

When I Drink From This Well

these warm waters soothe the tension
that holds me bound to yesterday

this ocean carries my body away
the warmth touching every ache

these unexplained mysteries
calling me awake –

the greatest freedom in life
comes when I let myself be

when I drink from this well
I am never thirsty

This Holy Labor

we give birth
day and night, night and day
each thought and feeling
our silent becoming

are we even conscious
of all the ways we nourish
or diminish

this holy labor

God In These Hands

I felt you there
in her silence.

I saw the miracle
even in her stillness.

no book could describe
no way to this knowing

God in these hands.

Sit By This Fire

in this rage
there is liberation

in this frustration
seeds of golden light

in this urge to shake your fist
the fire that galvanizes your spirit

let the flame be still
sit by this fire

where this and that
turns to ash

Nothing Has Healed Me More

you are why I keep on going
without you I'd be gone
nothing left to live for

in your eyes I see
the tremendous aliveness
the weight of what we've carried

nothing has healed me more
than your presence and your love
than knowing you are here

I Held

it's true
she died eight years ago

it's true
she was dead before she was born

it's true
she entered the world in silence

she was cold not warm
she was still not moving

it's true
I was devastated

but I was so proud of myself
I held the weight of our love

in my arms

Wholeheartedly Alive

when I die
I am not going to be
concerned with
books I have not read
refilling the toilet paper
washing the dishes
manicuring my nails
or brushing my hair

when I die
I am not going to
care about
supplements
progesterone levels
ovulation windows
going to yoga, or
tightening my ass

I won't care if people like me
approve, understand
or even love me

when I die
I'm not going to be
worried about
how much money I spend
or how badly I spell

I won't care
about pissing people off
or saying the appropriate
polite thing

when I die
I am not going to care about
instagram, facebook
twitter or tiktok
hashtags or likes

I'm not going
to care about
taking up space
playing it safe or
being enough

when I die
I am going to remember
every smile and hug
my daughter's little body
and the beautiful
gut wrenching silence
the love she gave to us
the morning she was born.

when I die
I am going to remember
my husband, his courage
my faith, our trust

my younger brother who cried
when I broke down in the living room
how my father held him and said
"it's okay mate, she just needs to feel this"

I will remember my mother
her strength, laughter and courage
and the cancer that came to take her home

I will remember the doctors that helped her
and the doctor who helped me too
the day Magnolia died

I will remember the nurses
and friends and strangers
who loved us

I will remember
these innocent eyes
that found beauty
in a place it did not belong

when I die
I will remember
the warmth of my husbands
body, his hands, breath and
those beautiful eyes
blue like a summer sky

I will remember
his kisses, our love making

and the wild joy of
being pregnant again

I will remember
our children
the sound of their laughter
the warmth of their little bodies
resting on mine

I will remember them growing
so quickly and thinking
how do I slow this down.

I will remember
the muffins we cooked
the shoelaces we tied
homework, movies
holidays, and the magnolia tree
in the front yard
on which we hung our prayers
on her birthday

when I die
I will remember
none of the worries
none of the fears
none of the pain

I will remember
again, and again
what a gift it was
to breathe, to walk
to run, to cry

what a gift it was
to be honestly, totally
wholeheartedly alive.

There Is Life

there is life
inside of this dying

there is joy
inside of this dying

there is beauty
mystery and pain
inside of this dying.

there is freedom
inside of this dying

there is perfection
inside of this dying

there is loss and
love and peace
inside of this dying

all I've strived for
lived my life for
it falls away

it falls away
inside of this dying

In My Veins

the body that held her
not the solid ground beneath my feet

the silky golden sand running through my fingers
nothing real, not her, just an image

never to be touched again.
but *she...*

she is eternal, *she* is the life
in my veins

When All Is Said and Done

when all is said and done
the sun will rise again
and I will walk outside
across the hardened concrete

the soft wet grass
will welcome these worn feet
and I will greet myself
as I did the day before.

when all is said and done,
these arms and lips that yearn to kiss
her tender face, and belly
will surprise me

I once thought
I'd never recover –
I now know
beyond a doubt
this was the answer
to my prayer.

God show me how to serve,
show me my place in this world.

and she came
like fire and water
and baptized every ache in me

and I held her
and she didn't move
and she didn't breathe
and she didn't speak
she ripped off the bandage

on the wound that would not heal
and in her absence taught me
how to love myself.

she holds me even now
telling me to let it come out,
no matter how painful.

when all is said and done,
the sun will rise again
and I will walk outside
across the hardened concrete

the soft wet grass
will welcome these worn feet
and I will greet myself
as I did the day before.

I once thought
I'd never recover –
I now know
beyond all doubt
she was the answer
to my prayer.

A Father's Thoughts

When I think about Magnolia, the first thing I wonder is if she, or her soul is truly connected to me as I feel or sometimes as I hope to believe it is. I wonder if she is looking over Libby and I and if her soul is really dancing amongst the others that include my parents, and Libby's mom. I have the belief that this happens, but I also have a skeptical brain that wonders if this is some kind of rational path to give me peace of mind. I also wonder at times if it's all a big dark nothing beyond this realm.

I think about my daughter who was here, then gone in a flash. I think about what it would have been like to see her grow, what she might have looked like and sounded like. What simple moments with her might have been like, such as playing the guitar for her, or going to the beach, or making a smoothie together, or imparting some of the wisdom and knowledge I've gained through my years.

It's an attractive notion to contemplate Magnolia, and then it's gone from my reality. A vacant flash that quickly turns to a sad melancholy that fills the space in my heart, and sometimes the room around me. It is no doubt an emptiness with a sad tone that cannot be erased, a tone of sadness that has always been a familiar part of me. I don't often let myself dwell on the acute trauma of the day when we lost her.

The moments that surround the loss are so slaying that they defy description. The emotional trauma was as acute and painful, beyond anything I could fathom. Mentally I was transported somewhere that most likely helped me to field the shock, do my part and take my role in supporting Libby, so we could survive this moment and what lay ahead.

All of the unknowns were a major anxiety for me. Would Libby be okay, would it hurt our marriage as such loss often does? To handle the anxiety in my head and the agony I felt in my heart I just did my job to hold space for the physical birth itself, and to keep Libby supported. I felt tremendous pain and empathy for her. She was working so hard to deliver our breathless baby that she got caught up in the ecstatic and empowering physicality of the delivery almost as a job itself to side step the horrific fact that our stillborn child was on her way.

Unlike Libby, who wanted to hold onto the birth and the experience as if it were a kind of high point within an immense tragedy (which it was for her an actual high point) all I could do to get through was embrace the notion that there was a teaching in this loss, and someday I would find it.

The moments that stand out to me are the phone call from Libby, saying we lost the baby, as if she were letting me or the world down. I bled for both of us in that moment.

The experience of holding Magnolia's body. Something I was afraid to do but on the encouragement of those in the room I did, and it carried a long-term bonding and healing affect.

I remember pushing the wheelchair through the maternity ward as Libby cradled Magnolia's body as if to somehow have a miracle happen and that she would awaken while all the parents around us celebrated the joy of their newborns.

During the labor I told my father and his wife who were crushed. I contemplated the conversation I couldn't have with my mom because she was in a long state of dementia and couldn't understand. As an only child who was close to my mom this was horrific. I still think how she would touch Libby's belly during the beautiful pregnancy without being able to form words in her demented state. A few days later on Thanksgiving I visited my mom in the nursing home and got the words out that we lost the baby. I cried, and she kind of stared into space unintelligibly. I showed her a photograph that our friend took on her phone of the moment she was born and all you can see in the image is a soft yellow white light. Our friend who is a spiritual guide to many said that that is when he felt the energy of her soul enter the room. Although this statement made us feel uplifted at the time it was short lived. In any case, I showed the photo to my mom, and in a flash these words leapt out of her mouth, the first legible sentence in a long time, "She's beautiful." I was dumbfounded.

The other moment I remember was handing Magnolia off to the coroner nurse with my mother-in-law Jo while Libby showered, preparing for us to go home. I can't even form the words for the feeling. At that point I was like a ghost carrying out physical duties which is how I stayed for some months. Only when Libby had major emotional outbursts and I would comfort her, was I able to feel the magnitude of my own grief and in those moments I too broke down.

The months that followed were so sad and heavy; with many births and celebrations happening in the world to friends and colleagues around us. We were now joined in a strange club that most of the world are not members of and cannot and hopefully will never know the loss and the extremity of its trauma. I recall the extreme difficulty for us to attempt integrating back into the world. For me my work didn't allow me much time beyond the Thanksgiving to Christmas season. I was so nervous to see acquaintances and people in the business whose first line was congratulations or show me a photo. Not knowing what they were about to hear. It caused me so much anxiety and in some instances shame.

I finally made the decision when asked about Magnolia at a restaurant we frequented in Venice, to lay out the words in succinct graphic simplicity. She died. It was an unforeseen complication. We are devastated.

The gift I received during this time was that the beautiful things in my life, which are plentiful, came into view in a new way. It's as if life got reframed and the beauty of it now had a bright spot light upon it. Our marriage deepened in profound ways and I am proud of how we came through this with a deep and precious bond. These are gifts as much as any gifts that I know. Make no mistake, in no way do they lessen the pain, loss or wounding that I carry. It was a slap on the hand as if to say your life is still magical and great and I see that vividly. It gave me a deeper connection to Libby and to what true gratitude is. The pain is the same. I drew upon what I learned in the moments when Libby felt that life was not worth living anymore. I never felt that way. But I didn't share the physicality of the loss.

Through this experience I've learned that it's possible to be vulnerable yet lead at the same time. In holding space for Libby I gained access to my own pain and an ability to love through this journey. New avenues of empathy and depths of learning opened for me, depths of compassion and love opened for me, dark corners of my psyche opened for me. Gradually, with time I began to embrace the grief that sat in my own being.

The depth of what I saw in my wife's grief, her writing, and her physical struggle allowed me to understand how deep these pains go, how much I felt them within myself, and how to access them. It made me understand the necessity of the dynamic of the male and female dance.

What I saw and observed in Libby that is often unacknowledged in females are the qualities of a warrior. To carry life and nurture it in your body, to put it forth into the world and then have it snuffed away – and to find your way back onto your feet is something that can't really be taught. In bearing witness to it I understand the power of the feminine, the resilience of the feminine, the fierceness and knowledge that is in the feminine about life; that the masculine can't quite carry unless it tunes into it.

I have always been in touch with the feminine qualities in myself. I am creative, I am inclined that way, but men are taught to be emotionless and strong, and it doesn't serve us. It doesn't serve our partnerships, and it doesn't serve the way the world has been working for a long time. Through this experience with Libby I began to see the scale and scope of what that means, much more than just trying to help heal the situation that we faced: to heal meant to be with it, to not turn away, run or fix it.

I found places of empathy and compassion in myself that were hidden in the guise of being a dude, or a strong enough person to conquer the things that we think we're supposed to conquer, like becoming successful at business, becoming a leader, becoming a man (traditionally what that has meant). I was able to find things through this journey, and so many of them were found by just sitting on the side of the bed, or on my knees whilst Libby lay there healing.

What I witnessed when Libby allowed herself to go all the way into the grief were depths of rage, frustration, despair, self-preservation, hope, faith, courage and resilience. She never gave up or succumbed to hiding, no matter how bloody it got. She didn't distract herself. She found a way to sit inside of it, thereby teaching me how to sit in it with her.

The other thing I've learned is that you're never going to replace what was lost. Magnolia will never be replaced. She's just going to run parallel, hopefully to another child that we have, or whatever happens. So often we are encouraged to "jump back into the game" as a way to try and move forward, which many people encouraged us to do, "you just need to try again" or "perhaps you guys should adopt."

And I knew it wouldn't have been right for us. This kind of "consoling" speaks to the collective inability to be with one another's grief, which is really just a reflection of our inability to be with our own.

I allowed Libby to be how she was. That's something I wasn't taught to do. My inclination in the past has been to fix it or distract to make things fun but it wasn't what was to be done. I knew that. I knew I couldn't take this away from her, I knew that I needed to let her have her process. I knew anything I tried to do to make it seem better would hinder her. I remember telling myself, *I don't have the power to bandage this.* Nobody does.

I understood that I couldn't take the pain away, that it was going to take time. I allowed time to happen and what happened within time was healing. I wanted to fix it but I knew I couldn't and that was such a paralyzing feeling.

When Magnolia was in the womb I developed a non-physical relationship with her. I created this relationship with her I suppose out of need. I didn't really have a physical relationship with Magnolia. Throughout the pregnancy I touched and kissed her through Libby's growing belly and it helped me put a visual label on it, but my experience of it was much more esoteric and still is.

Meeting her hammered home the reality of her existence and the physical loss. I didn't have any particular reward in that moment, but what it did was it made the reality of her brief life, her brief physical appearance real. It also gave depth to her spiritual existence, which I carry with me today. Holding her gave me something tangible to carry with me. As my relationship with her continues on a spiritual plane, I can see her as an entity, as a person, not just as an imaginary thing.

I still imagine in my spiritual relationship with her she's six, she's seven, she's running through the house, she's swimming in the pool her tiny arms wrapped around my neck, she's unwrapping things under the Christmas tree, I'm waiting outside school for her. I drop her off in the morning. I see those things spiritually.

Whether you've lost a child, a loved one, or something you held close to you like a career, I want to say that there is a way through it. And the deepest most profound way through it is by accessing what the loss *feels like*, more than what it means in your intellect. When we lose something we love, or an illness occurs there is a powerlessness in it, and the only thing that I've learned can help is to surrender to what is and to meet that moment with as much compassion and openness as possible.

Stephen

Epilogue

It hasn't been easy getting to the end of this book. In truth, there is a part of me that doesn't want to let it go. I am afraid that in letting go of this story I am letting go of Magnolia forever. This doesn't make any sense, given the scope of all I now know but to a part of me, these memories, feelings and images etched in my brain seem like all I will ever have of her– and to this part of me, letting go of the book means moving on, and moving on feels like another death. The only way I know to walk in peace anymore is to include this part of myself in my experience, the part that doesn't want to let go.

Healing is not getting over what happened. Healing is walking alongside what happened, making space for all that we feel. I know that now, deep in my bones. I also know that we can't do death alone, and we can't do grief alone, either. Bringing people into our experience has created compassion, connection and healing. So thank you for walking through these waters with us. Thank you for blessing each word with your gentle and loving eyes – and thank you for your open heart and the kindness with which you have turned each page.

It is hard to describe the gift that walking with Steve through the death of our daughter, my mother and now both his parents has been – there is an empathy present in our relationship that wasn't present before, and there is a recognition of something powerful happening below the surface of our human existence. We feel it when we slow down and pay attention – when we put aside our assumptions of what *should* be and open our hearts to *what* is.

For most of my life, I lived under the assumption that wholeness was a byproduct of being healed, and being healed meant not suffering, not experiencing grief or pain. I sought wholeness in the outside world, in productivity, accomplishment, and experience. I lived under the assumption that something outside of myself would alleviate my suffering. I didn't realize that the wholeness I sought would come through my willingness to sit in the discomfort, be with the hurt, and allow the full expression of the pain to move through me.

There are many gifts that have come through this time. I have found doorways to joy living alongside grief and the uncertainty of what lay ahead. I have learnt to yield to the circumstances, which are beyond my control – I have opened to a more empathetic existence with the parts of myself I found so hard to accept. The part needing to rest, and feel her feelings. The part needing to be held, and cared for. The part that wants to say no, and put herself first.

During this time of healing, I have learned to appreciate and honor the differences between how Steve and I have chosen to grieve. I have learned to not expect him to just open up to me. I have learned to listen, be patient and kind, and sensitive to his feelings and the timeline of how he wants to process his experience. I have also come to see how my busyness was a cover-up for the overwhelming feelings I was not willing to feel. I have learned to have compassion for the part of me that wants to be running around, accomplishing and producing because, underneath all of that, there is an anxious, person who never feels good enough, who is insecure, overwhelmed and terrified. During this time of healing I have learned how to be with the insecure, overwhelmed woman inside me. I have learned to slow down, rest, and love myself in a new way.

I came across some photos of my mum recently – pictures of her during her struggle with cancer. The image that especially touched me was captured the day my brother first shaved her hair off. She's sitting on the couch in a bright red sweater, blue skinny jeans, and a freshly buzzed head, beaming ear to ear, with a rebellious look on her face. I remember talking with her that day, and her saying, "Libby, I should have fucking done this years ago!"

Frustration, and grief were a big part of my mother's journey - but there was also a liberation that came alongside her suffering. I saw her take radical strides towards being more authentic. Some part of her knew that she couldn't wait anymore. The hours, minutes, and seconds were all she had left – and none of us had any idea how many she had. She started putting her needs first and saying what was on her mind. It was a shame it took a terminal illness for her to figure out that she never needed anyone's permission to live her life the way she pleased. But perhaps that was a huge part of her teaching – the wisdom she had come to impart on all those she knew and loved – to not wait to live our lives.

Being with my mother in the hospital and caring for her in the months leading up to her death reminded me that every second we get to live is a blessing. All we had in those final months were the glances and words passed back and forth between us and the experience of holding each other's hand. I walked alongside her for as long as I could, just as she had done for me.

Holding Magnolia's body in my arms, knowing that I would have to say goodbye to her, made the present moment more alive. It made my own life more valuable. Holding her, I knew that one day that would be me. Presence is the grace given in those final moments and the grace she gave to all of us that morning in the hospital.

The most memorable talk I had with my mum during her sickness was about dying. I remember sitting in her room in palliative care one day, and out of the blue, she said to me, "I want you to know, honey, that I am not afraid of dying." She continued, saying that in her meditations, she was becoming aware of herself as pure energy, an infinite energy not bound by this body. She described this energy as "a warm golden light" and said it felt "wonderful." She said she was "unafraid" because she was starting to realize this energy was "who she really was" and this energy "never ends." She said, "I am not afraid to die, because I am just opening and closing the door." When I asked her to tell me more, she said, "death is like opening a door and walking through to the other side. When I close my eyes, when I close that door, I will no longer be Joan. I will no longer be who I think I am but remember who I have always been – this energy that is everywhere and everything."

In the years that have unfolded since Magnolia and my mother's deaths, I have come to realize that I can choose to live each day in gratitude for the time I got to share with them, or I can dismantle my life and let everything I love fall to the wayside because of what happened to them.

I felt a tremendous weight lift from me the moment I realized that I didn't have to love what happened in order to accept it. From that moment forward, I started speaking more honestly about my experience. I allowed myself to share the anguish and depths of my despair. I chose to share with those I felt safest with, and sometimes I shared with complete strangers in my local coffee shop. I didn't care anymore about how I looked, the feelings were in there and I took every opportunity I had to get them out. I decided to reach out for help. This death was tearing me apart, but I knew if I could feel all the way into it, it would also tear me open.

Feeling the pain was an important part of my healing. It helped me become present. It supported me in becoming aware of the unconscious pressure I put on myself to try and make sense of the situation. It allowed me to move into a place of forgiveness for all the judgments and misperceptions I was carrying about what happened. The healing came when I finally gave myself permission to tend to my grief.

I would not be the person I am today had Magnolia lived. I am much more patient now. I have learned to honor the miracle of her birth and the healing that has come through her death. In the darkest moment of my life, I have learned to live with more depth of feeling, kindness, compassion, and honesty. In the shadow of the deepest pain I've ever known, lies more love than I ever knew possible.

It's been a long journey since that morning in the hospital and Steve and I are both beginning to understand the load we have carried these past few years and how all of the healing we have engaged in is preparing us for what's next. We're trying to figure out if parenting in the traditional sense is something that still calls to us, or if we are content in nurturing our spiritual relationship with Magnolia and the intimacy we have grown within ourselves.

I never could have imagined a day when I would question whether I still wanted to carry another child. But I've finally surrendered and I couldn't have arrived at this place any sooner, not while going through the experience of trying to become pregnant again; this was something that I had to get to on my own, with time.

I used to feel ashamed that I hadn't given birth to another child. Yet, the time I have taken to heal has shown me that my notions of motherhood and how and when it might happen needed to take a backseat so that I could reclaim the value in myself, and know that with or without another physical child I am still a mother. In the past few years I have taken the time to find out who I am when I'm not running around trying to be perfect. I've allowed myself to lay on the grass in my back yard and write poetry. I've graduated from a two-year master's program in Spiritual Psychology. I've studied healing movement practices, breath work, meditation, and sacred feminine dance. I've facilitated weekly poetry writing sessions, I've gone on road trips, and traveled farther inside myself. I never would have done any of this if Magnolia was here. I would have dissolved into her life – and probably never had the chance to look at any of my issues or heal the underlying hurts from my past.

I'm setting these words free now, knowing that in doing so I get to honor my daughter and the mother I have become – the one who has given birth to herself and an extraordinary life with her husband in the face of this loss.

My sincere gratitude, love and warmth for your journeying through these pages. May your life and the life of all those you love be infinitely blessed.

Libby

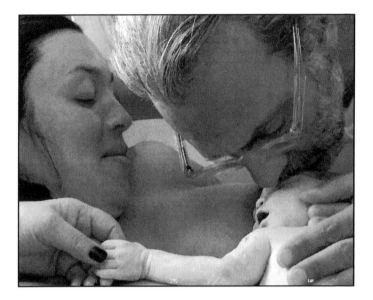

Moments after she was born.

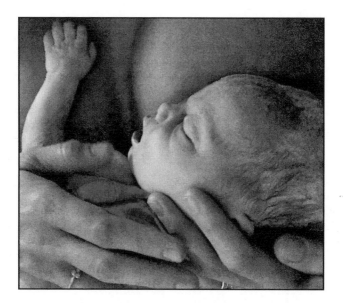

Magnolia Grace Weintraub.

My mother, Joan and Magnolia.

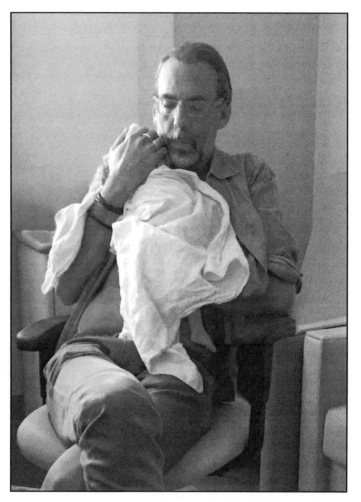

Steve and Magnolia.

Acknowledgments

I would like to thank everyone involved in bringing this work to life, but first and foremost, I want to acknowledge my husband our daughter, and the universal intelligence that has guided, loved and sustained us through this journey. Without them, these words would not exist.

Steve, nothing could have prepared us for this journey more than the love we share; it has been the base I have crawled my way back to in the darkest of hours, and while there were many nights I wanted to give up, you stood your ground and held me tight, knowing we would come through on the other side. Thank you for never giving up on us and for your words in this book that add so much honesty, insight, and healing to its message.

Thank you for your willingness to be vulnerable and for letting me see the dark ache of your grief. It helped me understand your process, needs, and how I could best hold space for you. I am grateful for the love, warmth, and compassion you have extended to me and for all the ways you have helped me find the strength to rise from the shattered pieces. You were why I kept going on the days I wanted my life to end.

It is the most incredible privilege of my life to love you, to walk by your side, and to have given birth to our beautiful baby Magnolia. Your devotion to your ongoing spiritual relationship with her moves me deeply. In my heart, I know how thankful and proud of you she is. Thank you for sharing your life with me. I love you, always.

Magnolia, my sweet angel, through your presence, I have learned what it is to love beyond measure and to accept the grace that comes in and through the uncertainties of life. You have broke us open and deepened our love. Your brief time here brought to the surface all that was still unresolved in our hearts, and throughout our healing, I have felt you by our side. Thank you for giving us this opportunity to learn how strong and capable we are. Thank you for trusting me to be your mother. I will hold you in my heart forever and spend the rest of my days looking for and welcoming your signs. I am the luckiest mother alive to have had you as long as I did. May your essence live on in the world through this book and in all the countless ways you already do. I love you endlessly, your mamma.

The following people are the midwives and doulas of this work. These words would not have seen the light of day without their invaluable contribution. They have stood by my side either in part or throughout the entire process of creating this book. They have given their time to help edit, shape, inspire, and encourage these words. I am eternally thankful to each of them. Elena Brower, Jasmine Golestaneh, Sophie Ward Koren, Reyna Sharp, Alisha Das, Angela Ai, Zofia Moreno, Renée Zellweger, Kaycee Flinn, Olivia Allen, Ever Pallas, Bruce Gelfand, Meredith Geller, Kate Rose, Nicole Trunfio, Pipsa Hurmerinta, Malissa Shriver, Ashleigh Erwin, Pauline Collinson, De Vie Weinstock, Farrah Summerford, Jack Grapes, and my love, Stephen Weintraub.

Ever Pallas, thank you for all of the preliminary work and the many hours it took to take the poems and contents of this book in its raw form and prepare it to be shaped into the book it has become. It has been an honor working with you. Your kindness and compassion are deeply appreciated.

James Benard and Kevin Sullivan at Benard Creative, thank you for your beautiful artful cover design, editing, and the finishing touches you added to the book's interior and images. I appreciate your generosity, time, and vision that has given life to this work. It has been a privilege working with you both.

Dylan Griffin, thank you for your extremely generous contribution to the cover. Your image captures the beauty, preciousness, and fragility of life, it speaks to that eternal place beyond the mind, and the possibility that there is life beyond this realm. Thank you for allowing me to use your photo on the cover; I am deeply touched.

Thank you to artist Joanna Szmerdt for permitting me to use your stunning magnolia-flower-Drawing in the pages of this book. Your work captures the essence of love in form, and you are a truly gifted artist.

Alisha Das, I am so grateful for the space you held in our sessions leading up to Magnolia's birth and for holding my hand during my labor and throughout my healing; I am immensely thankful for your friendship and the hours you have spent tending to my heart. Your guidance, love, insight, and prayers in the early days, and the years following Magnolia's death were invaluable to me in moving forward into the light of understanding.

Michael Hayes, thank you for holding such a powerful space for Steve and me during the early stages of my labor and throughout our healing process. You helped me to keep my eyes open to the teachings surfacing through our loss, and you assisted me in seeing that there was more unfolding beyond the trauma of what was taken.

To my teachers, doctors Mary R. Hulnick and H. Ronald Hulnick. When I entered your two-year master's program in Spiritual Psychology in 2012, I was searching for answers and a way forward. Deep below the surface of my life, I felt lost and was looking for a way to find peace, and I had no idea of the path ahead of me. Your work has been monumental in my healing. I'm endlessly grateful and blessed to have spent time in your classroom and in your presence. You have endowed me with a skill set that has helped me navigate the most frightening and challenging experience of my life. The work you have brought forth onto this planet is a blessing and a gift from God. Thank you for your service in moving humanity forward.

Johanna Jenkins, thank you for your ceaseless compassion and counsel in the early days. Your ability to hold space for healing to emerge in your sessions is laid in the foundation of your presence. I am so grateful to have worked with you.

Angela Ai, working with you has catalyzed a transformation I could never have imagined possible. You have given me a pathway into the darkness and held space for the unbridled expression of it in such a safe and sacred way. Thank you for helping me dig for the truth within myself and to look for the gold that was held within the path of allowing the rage and grief to pass through me. Your encouragement has been the wind at my back, pushing me forward since we met. I am grateful for the opportunity to work with you.

To my mother, Joan. I am sincerely grateful for the prayers, light, and love you shared with Steve and me in that darkened room during my labor and for bringing all the courage you could muster into that moment. Thank you for holding and comforting Steve when things got unbearable. I am overwhelmed by how you showed up for us both. I appreciate your willingness to sit in the discomfort and not try to fix me or make things better, trusting that I would get the answers in my own time. I imagine you raising Magnolia now in the unseen realms, holding her, and playing with her as I often dream. I love you, Mum.

I want to extend a warm embrace to our family members. For your sensitivity, understanding, compassion, and generosity. We could not have made it through without your support. To my father, Don; my brothers Troy and Domenic, and to Laura; our nieces Gabriela and Olivia, to Vicky, Lorraine, Dorothy, Guy, Mike, Iona, Amy, Tim, Danielle, and Sawyer. We are endlessly grateful to you all.

Zofia Moreno, thank you for saying yes to being Magnolia's Godmother. Thank you for keeping her essence alive by saying her name and sharing with me all the ways you experience her now in the unfolding of your days. Thank you for always being there. Your friendship lives inside of me.

Elena Brower and Sophie Ward Koren, thank you both for your deep listening and love. For picking up the phone and counseling me when I had doubts about sharing these words, when I couldn't see their value, and when I couldn't feel my own. I appreciate you both for pouring your enthusiasm into me and into every poem and for the time you invested in editing them. I am blessed to be on the receiving end of such unwavering friendship. Thank you.

Sheryl Crow, thank you for the tidal wave of love and care you poured into Steve and me during our recovery. Your calls of support and the weeks of nourishing meals you sent to our doorstep made our lives during those devastating first few weeks much easier and more manageable. Thank you also for reading the book and for your words of support and encouragement.

Pam Wertheimer, Pam Adams and Nicole Avena, we are deeply indebted to you for the love and care you showered upon us in those early days so we could continue resting and nesting into our healing. We are sincerely grateful to have you in our close inner circle and are so thankful for you holding down the fort during the first critical year of our healing.

Thank you to our friends and extended family for holding space for our grief, sending cards, flowers, and notes, checking in on Mother's and Father's Day, and reaching out on Magnolia's birthday. It means the world to us. We appreciate your encouragement and for taking the time to listen and support us; it means more than I can ever say: Desiree Gruber, Callum and Kyle MacLauchlan, Cassy Britton, Lola Delon, Massimo Cuviello, Rebecca Sharzer, Pipsa Hurmerinta, Elena Brower, Chloe Crespi, Paige Stewart, Lysa Cooper, Kate, and Tim McGregor. Pam Adams, Nicole Avena, Pam Wertheimer, Richard and Lauree Volpe, Todd Wolfe, Anu and Ariel Krys, Meredith Geller, Hailey Gates, Pauline Collinson, Robert and Jacqui Fein, Melissa Shangold, Kate Rose, Nicole Trunfio, Gary Clark Jr, Gary Clark Sr, and Sandy Clark. Shayla Scuffi, Bobby and Melissa Shriver, Mark and Megan Dowely, Mitch Glazer, Kelly Lynch, Raquel Horn, Damon Dash, Shannon Fraser Butler, Teresa, and Christoph Jouany. Zofia, Jean, Cielo, and Dean Moreno. Kaycee Flinn, Renée Zellweger, Olivia Allen, Harriet Kaiser, Jacquie and Ira Rosen, Baelyn Neff, Annah Taylor Phinny, Linda Wolff, Clarence Greenwood, Alice Smith, and Lula. Isaac, Jules, and Sophie Koren. Thorald and Ashley Koren, Rena Small, Roger and Denise Behle, Sue and Paud Stemp, Mark Palmen, James and Drew Gardner. Alicia Drake, Roy Pachinskey, Melissa Harris, Andy Slater, Lida Ahmady, Larry Yellen, and Elaine. Elizabeth George, Jennifer Grabber, and Arya. Jessica Sharzer, Jon Rubin, Kathleen Vizconde, Kathleen Graham, Kelsey Bunce, Kris Wolcott, and Lindsey Hively McKeon. Ele Keates, Nadia Mitri, Brittney and Lisset Gallego King, Alia Lahlou, and Shona O'Neill.

An enormous thank you and many blessings to all the healers and practitioners involved in our journey; my midwife Aleksandra Evanguelidi, Giuditta Tornetta, Dr. Daoshing Ni, Dr. Elliot Berlin, Dr. Howard Mandel, Dr. Stuart Fischbein, Drs. Ron and Mary Hulnick. Abdi Assadi, Johanna Jenkins, Dr. Kumiko Yammamoto, Dr. Habib Sadeghi, Dr. Dawn Desylvia, Marta and Roger Soffer at Surya Spa, Angela Ai, and Dr. Sara Koorjee.

Denise and Roger Behle, we are grateful for your love, kindness, friendship, and support. Roger, thank you for securing the copyright for this book. I am so thankful to have your care and enthusiasm woven into its energy.

In closing, I would like to thank the fierce clan of parents Steve, and I belong to, those of us who have loved and let go of our babies long before we ever imagined having to. I bow at your feet in reverence and respect.

Resources — Books

The following collection of books have inspired strength, supported insight and offered hope to me on my journey. I share them here should you desire to lean into the powerful medicine contained within their pages.

It's OK That You're Not OK: Meeting Grief and Loss in a Culture That Doesn't Understand. Megan Devine

Beneath All Appearances: an unwavering peace. Rashani Rea, Rosemerry Wahtola Trommer & Damascena Tani

Once More We Saw Stars. Jayson Greene

Still: A Memoir of Love, Loss, and Motherhood. Emma Hansen

Stars at Night: When Darkness Unfolds as Light. Paula D'Arcy

Signs: The Secret Language of the Universe. Laura Lynne Jackson

Beyond Grief, Navigating the Journey of Pregnancy and Baby Loss. Pippa Vosper

Inward. Yung Pueblo

Loyalty to Your Soul: The Heart of Spiritual Psychology. H. Ronald Hulnick, Ph.D. and Mary R. Hulnick, Ph.D.

Loving What Is: Four Questions That Can Change Your Life. Byron Katie with Stephen Mitchell

Resources — Organizations

The following organizations continue to provide much needed support to parents and their family members who have suffered the loss of a child.

Refuge in Grief –
Was founded by Megan Devine a psychotherapist, writer, grief advocate, & communication expert. Megan has built her life around helping people through some of the worst times of their lives and her book *It's Okay That You're Not Ok, Meeting Grief and Loss in a Culture That Doesn't Understand* isn't your typical book on loss. It's a whole new way to look at grief – and love. Megan facilitates a 30-day writing course that lets people tell the truth about their grief. Her website: https://refugeingrief.com/

The MISS Foundation –
Established in 1996 by Dr. Joanne Cacciatore, is an international 501(c)3, volunteer-based organization providing C.A.R.E. [counseling, advocacy, research, and education] services to families experiencing the death of a child. They recognize that the death of a child at any age is one of life's most tragic experiences. Their website: https://www.missfoundation.org/

Share Pregnancy & Infant Loss Support, Inc –
The mission of Share Pregnancy & Infant Loss Support, Inc. is to serve those whose lives are touched by the death of a baby through pregnancy loss, stillbirth, or in the first few months of life. The primary purpose is to provide support experienced at the time of, or following the death of a baby. This support encompasses emotional, physical, spiritual and social healing, as well as sustaining the family unit. The secondary purpose is to provide information, education, and resources on the needs and rights

of bereaved parents and siblings. The objective is to aid those in the community, including family, friends, employers, members of the congregation, caregivers, professionals, and others in a supportive role. Their website: https://nationalshare.org/

The TEARS Foundation –
The TEARS Foundation is a 501(c)(3) non-profit organization that seeks to compassionately assist bereaved parents with the financial expenses they face in making final arrangements for their precious baby who has died. Many of the founders and volunteers at The TEARS Foundation have experienced the loss of their own baby, and want to reach out in this way to support newly bereaved parents in their time of devastating sorrow. Their website: https://thetearsfoundation.org/

The Dougy Center –
The Dougy Center are world-renowned for their expertise and approach to childhood bereavement, providing support in a safe environment where children, teens, young adults, and their families grieving a death can share their experiences. All Dougy Center programs offer support to families at no cost. They are supported solely through private support from individuals, foundations and companies. You can find them here at their website: https://www.dougy.org/

Hayden's Helping Hands –
Hayden's Helping Hands was founded by Rebekka and Randy Hauskins in 2010, after experiencing the loss of their daughter Hayden Ruth who was stillborn at 32 weeks of gestation. Hayden's Helping Hands is a non-profit foundation who helps U.S. families in the midst of tragedy. They assist families after the birth of a stillborn baby by paying for a portion of their hospital delivery expenses. The founders of

this non-profit, continue to bring light to so many through the loving memory of their daughter Hayden Ruth. Their website: https://www.haydenshelpinghands.com/

Still Standing Magazine –
Founded in 2012, Still Standing Magazine has been the world's leading online voice in breaking the silence on child loss – from conception to adulthood, and infertility. They share stories from around the world of writers surviving the aftermath of loss and grief – and include information on how others can help. This is a page for all grieving parents. If you grieve the loss of your child, no matter the circumstances, you are welcome. Their website: https://stillstandingmag.com/category/stillbirth/

About the Author

Libby June Weintraub is a mother, artist, writer, and poet. She was born in Western Australia and now lives in Santa Monica California with her husband Stephen (Scooter) Weintraub. In 2014, she gave birth to their stillborn child, Magnolia Grace. *She was Born: Words on Loss and Liberation* is her first book, a collection of poems that have supported a path of healing. It is her hope that these words offer comfort, especially to those who have known the devastation of losing a child.

Contact Information:
www.libbyjuneweintraub.com
@libbyjuneweintraub